How to Analyze People

I0414268

The Art of Reading Body Language

The Underground Playbook for Analyzing People

Alfred Smith

Contents

Introduction

Are you a man who is wondering whether or not a particular woman is interested in you? Are you a woman who is wondering the same thing about a man? Love can be quite awkward in the beginning when we just don't know whether that interesting person feels the same way about us as we do about them. Sometimes we read people correctly, and other times we don't.

This book is the second book in a series on the subject of reading people through body language.

In the first book, we discussed categorizing people by personality type and their known background. We discussed profiling techniques and nine things that FBI agents do when they read people. We looked at the many visual and audible cues people give, including word choices and cues that indicate the person is lying. We also discussed formal personality tests that are available.

The emphasis in this book is on reading romantic cues. We will also discuss how men and women send signals to each other with their body language and also how couples tell others about their relationship through their combined body language.

We will also review the personality types and the general body language cues, explore how perception colors our view of what we see, look at some of the different ways people respond to what they perceive is being said with body language, and discuss the rewards of reading people correctly.

Let's take a look.

Chapter 1: Personality Types

This chapter briefly reviews the four personality types and the combination ones that we discussed in more detail in the first book in this series.

If you notice, there are certain types of people that you find working in different types of jobs. Sometimes people are not in their element and it shows, while other people shine doing the same job.

Some employers have personality tests administered to candidates so that the employer can know whether or not the candidate fits the mold of the kind of person they need to fill the job vacancy.

In one's personal life, how often have we heard a man say, "She's not my type," or a woman say, "He's not my type," when evaluating someone as a potential lover, spouse, etc.? We judge people to be of a certain type that we instinctively know we are either compatible with or incompatible with, generally speaking.

Sometimes just the person's appearance is what we think we are evaluating, but the appearance often reflects something about what the personality is.

The Four Main Personality Types

The Leader – These are the confident ones who love to be in charge. They are serious people of strong words and demeanor who pace the floor and gesture with their hands when speaking to groups. They are also decisive, quick thinkers who are usually energetic. People naturally follow them.

They love money, and all that money buys them, including a trophy wife, and they view family and relationships second in importance to making money.

A well-known example of this personality type is President Trump. Love him or hate him, many video clips over the years show him talking endlessly about money. Video clips also exist that show his marital problems over the years and an unusual coolness and even disrespect toward his current beautiful trophy wife, Melania.

The Fraternizer – These are the outgoing, friendly people who command a presence in any room. They speak their mind with ease, spreading their optimism and enthusiasm everywhere.

You will find this type of person in jobs that require them to deal with people individually, such as in sales or event planner positions. They love fun and taking risks. They also love to travel and participate in outdoor activities and group gatherings.

These are fun people to have a relationship with, although they may try to "wear a mask" when you first meet them, trying to be what they think is a more impressive person. A lot of entertainers have this personality type.

The Identifier – These are the people who sit back and listen. You will find them asking open-ended questions which require the other person to say more than "yes" or "no." Their body language is relaxed and open.

They like in-depth discussions and building relationships that are based on trust. Relationships are more important to them than anything else. They are helpful, compassionate people who are commonly found working as nurses, teachers, counselors, caregivers, etc.

The Perceiver – These are the cautious types who like clarity and order in both their conversations and in their relationships. They often appear to be serious or stressed out. Their body language shows them to be closed, often crossing their arms, and you will think them to be standoffish when you meet them. When you get to know them, you will find them to be the dependable ones in the group.

They are analytical thinkers and prefer to talk to you about educational topics or about facts or theories on any non-emotional subject. They work alone in engineering, mathematics, technology or science. Their friendships are with other people who have a need for stability and structure.

The Combination Personality Types

To figure out combination people, you'll need first to find the dominant personality. You do this by observing the most obvious characteristics of facial expressions, body language, the manner of speaking (do they say "I" a lot or disallow others to speak?). Observe how they make you feel. Then observe any secondary personality traits to figure out if they have a combination personality and which type of secondary personality they have.

The Leader-Fraternizer – These people will be easy to figure out because they really stand out in a crowd, being sociable and energetic while also being leaders. These types can become highly successful.

They view every goal as attainable, and they tend to be fantastic motivational speakers and successful entrepreneurs. These people are highly tuned into how the people around them feel about things and will fight for causes.

The Leader-Identifier – These people are rare, but you will know them by their ability to both lead and mentor. They are the bosses that you can talk to behind closed doors and really be listened to.

These leaders find success through their ability to read people and situations quickly, taking few risks, and through their ability to build trust. You'll find them working as marketing representatives or as directors of Human Resources departments.

The Leader-Perceiver – These are the successful, goal-oriented leaders who are hard to get to know on a personal level because they are all business. They also work along with data and facts, so they tend to work in science or technology careers.

They surround themselves with other people who keep emotions out of their conversations because that is what makes them more comfortable. They think before they speak, so they are rarely involved in arguments.

The Fraternizer-Identifier – This is a rare personality type. These people like to fraternize and to be cheerful, but they also have a decreased energy level. They dislike conflict, and they fit into most social and professional settings.

DISC Labeling

The four main personality types can also be labeled as being dominant, influential, steady or conscientious.

Dominant – The DISC system states that dominant people are opinionated, blunt, competitive, innovative, adventurous, vocal, and demanding people who are pioneers in their professions.

These people are in a hurry and will even interrupt people so as to dominate conversations in the direction they want it to go, especially if the people they are interrupting are making a lot of small talks.

Influential – Influential people are labeled as positive, friendly, open, excited, fun, communicative, social and influential. They dominate conversations, sometimes getting off of the topic. They also sometimes violate one's personal space.

Steady – Steady people are described as methodical, deliberate, and stable. They get all of the facts before they make decisions. They are quiet listeners who aren't very animated when they do speak but talk too much about details when they talk.

Conscientious – Conscientious people are logical and precise rule followers. They strive so hard to be perfect that they are critical of themselves. These people prefer to write rather than to speak, which makes them seem to be cold people when they actually aren't. They talk about facts more than about feelings, and they don't like to be wrong or to get into arguments with others.

Chapter 2: Perception

Perception is intuitive or immediate recognition. How we perceive has been debated for thousands of years, but it seems to come down to our backgrounds. That is because our life experiences and the culture we come from color how we perceive what we see.

Culture differences between the East and the West are particularly different from each other, which contributes to a misunderstanding of intentions when one of them observes the other.

It is helpful, then, to have skill in the art of communication so that we can be more open to the idea that our interpretations or perceptions of things could be wrong. Ongoing feedback helps us to get a clear understanding.

Body Language and Image

What things do we in Western culture notice about each other that quickly form our impressions of each other? We notice the following things:

- Posture, whether slouching or sitting up straight
- Walking and standing manner
- Overall body language, whether open or closed
- Facial expression warmth and appropriateness
- Gesturing, whether distracting or appropriate
- Fidgeting
- Thoughtfulness/energy balance to what is being said
- Grooming/cleanliness, clothing and hair styles, and makeup

Perceptive people can also sense a person's level of self-confidence and their general outlook, whether positive or negative.

Studies done at Stanford University show us that 55% of what we communicate is through body language and that only 7% of communication comes from our actual words and 38% comes from our tone of voice.

When what is said verbally does not match what is said through the body language, we perceive the body language to be telling the truth. Thus, many liars and/or flatterers think they are crafty, when, all the while, their own body language is telling off on them!

Still, it would be wise to observe many factors over time to more correctly read that person.

We often see ourselves through the feedback we get from others. Since the perception that others have of us or our intentions may be off, their misconceptions may cause our self-perception not to be accurate as well. Harming another person's sense of self-worth through harsh words or critical looks is one reason why people should be careful of what they communicate to others.

First Impressions

When we meet someone, research shows that it only takes between three and seven seconds for us to form an impression of that person. If that person makes a negative impression, it takes a lot more time for us to change the negative impression we have of that person to a positive one.

Given just a little more time, we can quickly form even more lasting impressions. For instance, if the other person does not listen to you very closely, that is a big negative thing because it usually indicates that what you have to say is unimportant to him. Does he even remember your name?

You likely won't soon forget being made to feel unimportant, and you certainly won't come back for more abuse if you can help it.

Misconceptions

It is possible, however, that the person was distracted by something about you when you were talking. For instance, maybe your eyes and/or your manner of speaking captivated that person, temporarily distracting him from paying attention to what you were saying.

For him, it could have been "love at first sight," and what appeared to you to be disinterest could actually have been intense interest! This sort of misconception on your part will become evident rather quickly when you notice they keep talking to you.

Consider also that a person could be terribly attracted to you but is too shy to talk to you much at all until they have had time to get to know you and feel comfortable talking to you. This could develop into a very healthy, long-term relationship.

A person could be attracted to you but is married or engaged to somebody or is otherwise emotionally unavailable.

Conversely, a wildly sociable person (maybe a "fraternizer" type discussed in Chapter 1) could impress you as being really interested in you, and then you find that they were just as friendly toward you as they are with everybody else.

Sometimes you meet a Casanova type of person who has lovers everywhere they go! At first, you think you have a whirlwind romance with that person, just to discover that you are just one of his many love interests and that you have been getting played for a fool. These people don't even have to be good looking to have this game in place.

These people are frequently away from you, making it easy for them to have a love interest elsewhere while carrying on with you where you live. Surprise them at one of their other hangouts and their deceit will quickly be found out!

Time will sort out all of these kinds of things. Nevertheless, we do tend to form first impressions (perceptions) of each other rather quickly.

Chapter 3: How to Read Body Language

The ability to read body language is quite a useful skill to have. It is so useful that both lawyers and law enforcement people learn and use them in the course of performing their jobs when getting to the truth of situations is important.

Imagine how useful this skill would be to employers who conduct interviews or to salespeople who need to know what the maximum price is they can get out of a prospective buyer, etc.

When a man or a woman is attracted to the other, this skill will save some embarrassing moments when one of the parties is uninterested or is unavailable, and it would speed up the process if both parties are attracted.

This skill is useful for anyone who cares to know what is going on inside of another person's head so that they can adapt their message and/or make good decisions concerning the person who is being read.

The lists in this chapter are, for the most part, a recap of the first book, but with an emphasis on the (body) language of love. There are a few things a person should keep in mind, however, when utilizing the list of mannerisms that are associated with the various emotions.

Create a Baseline

It is important to create a baseline for a person who is being read, however, so as to enable reading that person more accurately. People have quirks to their personalities where they often make particular gestures, cross their arms, look at the floor, pout, wiggle their feet, stroke their neck, scratch their head, etc. These gestures could be misconstrued as lying or as something else if one does not know that the person makes those same gestures during unthreatening times.

To establish a baseline, all one has to do is to ask that person non-threatening questions that they have no reason to lie about and notate what their mannerisms are. These are the mannerisms that can, for the most part, be discounted when asking them stressful questions later on. Also, if you know they are feeling nervous or some other way, make a mental note what their mannerisms are under the various known states of mind.

Take Note of Clusters of Gestures

Certain gestures and other types of body language indicate particular emotions. The exhibition of one of them can be dismissed as normal for a person if previously found to be just a baseline mannerism, but if that person displays many of the cues for lying or for something else, pay attention to the emotion that the cluster of gestures indicates.

Compare and Contrast

Does the behavior change when some other person enters the room or when something else about a situation changes?

Mirrored Actions

When we smile at a person, it is normal for that person to smile back. If normal reciprocity is ignored, they are likely sending you the message that they do not like you or that they do not like something that you did. We'll get into this one in more detail in another chapter.

Find the Strong Voice

There may be a loud, obnoxious person in the room, but they may not be the one that the people are following. It just might be a more reserved, confident individual who is in the same room that you will find is the unofficial leader.

Watch their Walk

A person's confidence level is in their walk. Shuffling along, walking without a flowing kind of motion, or walking with their head down shows a lack of confidence.

Word Choice

Listen to the person's more meaningful words, such as "decided." "Decided" indicates that the person looked at several options and thought about the various options before they made a decision rather than acting under impulse.

Figure Out Their Personality Type

What feeds the person's ego? Is the person an extrovert or an introvert? How does that person act when they are under stress?

General, Non-Couple Visual and Audible Cues

The Visual Cues

General Body Language

Adam's Apple jumping – Under stress; embarrassed; anxious

Sitting, leaning back in chair – Closed off; false statement

Sitting, straight with shoulders back – Confident

Sitting, poor posture – Unconfident

Mirroring your actions – Building rapport with you

Expression limited overall – False statement

Fidgeting – False statement

Proximity, close physical – Affection

Rearranging self – False statement

Space between them and lower status person – Demonstrating power and dominance

Stance, tall and wide – Establishing dominance

Sitting vs. Standing – Establishing dominance if standing

Turning body away from person – Uncomfortable with accuser/questioner

Walking in front of others – Establishing dominance

Eyebrows

Raised quickly – Expressing congeniality, sending clear communication signal

V-shaped – At a threatening stage or even angry

Eyes

Blinking, much – Eye blocking; disbelief or disagreement; anxious; lying

Blinking, slowly – Sleepy or bored

Closing eyes while speaking - Avoiding looking at you, may be lying

Contact, avoidance – May be lying

Contact, constant – Trying to intimidate or threaten; communicating dominance

Contact, 80% of time while conversing – Interested in conversation; aware of their message; truthful; trying to cover up lying

Crinkling – Threatening or angry

Crying – Grieving, sad; laughing hard; very happy

Darting – Wanting to escape, insecure

Gazing, long – Deeply interested in the person; Displaying disagreement with superior

Gazing, lowering – Shy, timid; upset, hiding emotions; feeling unpleasant; embarrassed; closed

Gazing, avoid – Uncomfortable; lying

Gazing, regularly – Encouraging to like them; open

Gazing, social – Comfortable, looking between the eyes and mouth

Gazing, power – Looking between eyes and forehead

Glancing, sideways – Uncertain; need more information

Glancing, sideways (and with furrowed brows) – Critical, suspicious

Glancing, intermittently for a long time – Possibly interested in the conversation

Looking to the side while speaking – Avoiding looking at you, may be lying

Looking to the left – Audio creation in their mind

Looking to the right – Audio remembering

Looking away – Curious about surroundings; shy; interested in your other movements;   could be attracted to you

Looking down, then to the left – Smell, feel or taste remembering

Looking down, then to the right – Inner dialogue, possibly creating a story

Looking up, then to the right while speaking –
You've been dismissed and/or they are bored.

Looking up, then to the right – Visual
remembering

Looking up, then to the left – Visual construction
of an image in their mind

Looking over glasses – Trying to intimidate you

Pupils small – Offended; in bright light

Pupils dilated – Stimulated by what they see; in
low light; on some sort of substance

Rolling upwards – Exasperation if dramatically
done; showing disagreement

Rubbing – Eye blocking; disbelief; disagreement;
showing consternation; lying

Squinting while conversing – Suspicious; not
liking what you say

Widening – Threatening or angry

Nose

Flared – Angry or agitated

Twisted to side – Disliking or disagreeing

Wrinkled – Repulsed

Mouth

Nail biting – Anxious

Lip biting – About to make a false statement

Down-turned or open – Threatening or angry

Pursing while narrowing eyes – Mad

Pursing – Communicating seriousness; establishing dominance

Facial Expression

Gulping/difficulty swallowing – False statement

Smiling asymmetrically – False statement

Smiling, small – Full of pride

Smiling, including eyes – Genuine happiness

Smiling, not including eyes – Faking happiness

Smiling too long – Nervous or lying; super happy; attracted

Smiling while talking – True statement

Smiling after talking – False statement

Smiling unnaturally – False statement

Uncharacteristic emotion – False statement

Expression does not match words spoken – False statement

Expressions limited, not matching spoken expression – False statement

Frowning – Communicating seriousness; establishing dominance

Blushing – Feeling insecure

Sweating – Feeling insecure; possibly making a false statement

Asymmetrical movements, increasing – Anxious

Gesturing

Drumming fingers – False statement

First physical reaction doesn't match words spoken – False statement

Gestures don't match emotion (emotion too long or delayed, then stopped) – False statement

Gesture duration off – False statement

Gestures nonempathetic – False statement

Touching hair – Your opinion matters; possible romantic interest

Twirling hair – Nervous; possible romantic interest

Combing hair – Nervous/fearful of lie being detected, manipulating a body part

Touching face – False statement

Touching or scratching nose – False statement

Touching nose while talking – Concealing something

Touching mouth – False statement

Touching or scratching behind ear – False statement

Scratching ear – False statement; lacking confidence

Touching face often – False statement, especially if touching their lips.

Rubbing chin with forefinger – Doubting you

Stroking chin – Pensive; interested

Holding chin – Faking interest; bored

Touching throat – False statement

Hands on heart – Truthful statement; heartfelt statement

Hands on hips – Full of pride

Hands in pockets, thumbs out – Conveying superiority; confident

Hands showing thumbs – Conveying superiority

Hands fidgeting – Anxious

Hands, palms up – Open; possibly romantic

Hands placing objects in between them and you – False statement

Hands hidden – False statement; uncommunicative

Hands, large gestures – Conveying dominance

Handshake, long and firm with hand on top – Conveying dominance

Handshake, bone-crunching – Conveying dominance; enthusiastic

Handshake, double – Inviting intimacy or trust; friendly

Manipulates their jaw – False statement

Waving, open-handed – Welcoming and inviting

Rubbing forehead – False statement

Rubbing back of neck – False statement

Smoothing clothes continually – Shows behavior of a liar

Touching nearby objects continually – Bending, folding, twisting over and over shows behavior of a liar

Touch avoidance of person normally touched – False statement

Trembling – False statement

Head

Level – Authoritative, Confident

Movement backward – False statement

Nodding – Interested in conversation

Shaking – Disbelieving; disagreeing

Tilted – Thinking of how to answer question; paying attention

Tilted back slightly – Full of pride

Arms and Legs

Arms behind neck/head – Laid back; open

Arms crossed – Threatening or angry; insecure; closed; may lie to you

Legs crossed – Threatening or angry; insecure; closed; may lie to you

Legs, jittery – Anxious

Legs movement inward – False statement

Feet

Feet pointing away – Closed

Feet tapping – Anxious

The Audible Cues

Speaking Tones

Clears throat – False statement

Speaking plainly – Normal

Speaking sarcastically to avoid subject – Frustrated; to insult; to shut down argument; to establish power differences; to underline solidarity with audience; possibly lying

Speaking with suspense – Putting you into suspense

Speaking of humor to avoid subject – Could be lying

Speaking sadly – Sad

Speaking excitedly – Excited

Stammering – Insecure

Speaks in monotonous tone, with little emphasis – Likely lying

Garbled words – Likely lying

Speaks softly – Likely lying

Speaking Pace

Fast pace – Excited

Slow pace – Mentally slow; tired; laid back

Word Repetition

Repetition of words – Emphasizing statement; clarifying

Repetition of your question in his answer – Likely lying

Verbal Content

Defensive talk – Likely lying

Offensive talk – Likely telling the truth

Uses contractions ("it's" for "it is") – Likely telling the truth

Uses conjunctions a lot – False statement

Uses prepositions a lot – False statement

Uses "we" a lot and avoids saying "I" – False statement

Makes passive statements instead of direct ones – Being deceptive

Implies answers, not directly speaking them – Likely lying

Makes direct statements- Likely telling the truth

Talks too much (adds unnecessary details and uncomfortable with pauses in conversation) – Likely lying to you

Speaking with grammar/syntax wrong – False statement

Omits pronouns (he, she, etc.) – Likely lying

Gladly changes subject along with you – Likely has been lying

Chapter 4: Mirroring

Mirroring is the act of copying what another person does with some part of their body. Mirroring another person's body language is usually an unconscious thing that we do, but it results in subtly building understanding, a bond, and a mutual trust. It is often done in the form of smiling and yawning, but it can include other parts of the body.

Creating an environment through music or some other way can bring people together mentally, which then brings about the subconscious mirroring behavior and then the bonding that follows. You will see people at concerts acting in similar ways, maybe swaying their arms in the air to the left and then to the right together and to the beat of the song. A date may put on some soft music to affect the mood of the other person.

One can affect their own mood by assuming certain facial expressions or physical stances that convey feelings that they do not yet feel. After a while, they do feel that way. People plaster a fake smile on their faces and eventually feel happy.

People stand as if they are confident when they really aren't confident, but they later become confident because of assuming the pose. In conversation, while seated, people will make themselves confident by making a church steeple with their forefingers.

Women recognize body language easier than men do and women mirror body language more often than men do. If a man mirrors a woman's facial expressions while she is talking, she will consider him to be intelligent, caring and even attractive.

However, men prefer to hide behind masks and not display their emotions, at least with their faces, so that they feel they are in control of whatever the situation is. A man's expression of his attitudes is in his body, so to mirror a man, a woman needs to use less facial expression. If you don't do that, he will consider you to be intimidating.

Don't guess what he is feeling and then mirror that because you would appear silly. Keep a straight face in business situations, and you will appear to be smart.

Mirroring can also be done with voices, accents, and intonations. Don't speak faster than the other person because you would make that person feel pressure. Speak at the same pace or slower. Couple voice is mirroring with physical mirroring, and you will build trust and understanding.

Don't mirror a person who is above you in rank, such as your boss, or he will actually think you are arrogant. However, you can use it to disarm people who are pretending to be superior to you.

This technique works best for establishing a connection or rapport with new people. If you meet a person you are attracted to, or you are a marketer/salesperson, mimicking that person you are trying to connect to increases the chances they will like you. It is a form of flirting. Copy their sitting position, posture, gestures, talking pace and tone of voice, the drink or appetizer they order, and they will think there is just something they really like about you. You are in sync with the other person.

Chapter 5: Body Language Psychology

The psychology of body language is interesting to study. It can also be a useful tool. While mirroring is a powerful tool, so is the power of suggestion. The power of suggestion can be verbal or physical (through body language).

Verbal Power of Suggestion

We'll just touch on this one briefly since we are focusing on body language in this book.

The verbal power of suggestion is common practice when raising a child and telling him or her that they are "good" or that they "don't want" whatever the bad outcome might be if they were to do a particular thing, etc.

It has been said that phobias sometimes form through some verbal power of suggestion that was repeated. Interesting.

Sometimes a person tells another person that some medical procedure hurts. Then the person frets about their upcoming procedure, expecting it to hurt. They may even believe it had hurt after the experience when it didn't hurt. Sometimes the fear mongering prevents a person from having a needed procedure. What a shame.

Physical Power of Suggestion

We've noticed that when a person we are talking to gets up to leave a conversation that we get up too. When a person walks to the door, opens it and makes parting words to you, you automatically leave.

The physical power of suggestion also opens many doors, both literally and figuratively.

Salesforce example - In sales school training programs for door-to-door health insurance sales agents, a physical power of suggestion (body language psychology) technique is actually taught to get the sales force welcomed into a stranger's home.

How it works is that the sales person tells the homeowner they want to discuss the person's personal health situation or something similar. Then they break eye contact with the homeowner and look down at their feet and wipe their feet, whether or not a door mat is there.

The act of wiping their feet is what a respectable person may do before they enter a clean house. Psychologically, the homeowner connects the act of wiping feet with the polite stranger already being in the process of coming in the door. The homeowner automatically opens the door, steps aside and lets the stranger in.

Then the sales agent chats them up, and the homeowner finally discovers that the stranger was a crafty insurance sales person who had managed to trick them into letting them into their home. Of course, that part doesn't sit well with people, but the fact that a person can get into almost any home with the feet wiping act is scary!

This particular act works on about 19 out of every 20 people. I know this from personal experience as a door-to-door cancer insurance sales person.

However, I witnessed my trainer unable to get into this one really old woman's home. It was hilarious to watch the home owner watch my trainer wipe her feet and then not move aside and open the door! Unaffected, the old woman just casually looked down at my trainer's shoes as if she was just observing somebody on her front porch acting weird. She didn't move an inch. I had to laugh. My trainer could normally access any home and sell to almost everyone, but not there!

Criminals example - It's bad enough that we often unlock and open doors without looking to see who is there first, but body language/physical power of suggestion makes some people open their door for criminals, which is no laughing matter.

Criminals sometimes gain easy entry through a bologna story and some form of body language, the power of suggestion, or a prop such as a cop's uniform. An easier prop would be a hot pizza that they just need to get to a customer whose house they can't find and they "need" to use the homeowner's phone. All that criminal spokesman would have to do is be clean cut and non-threateningly normal looking, appear to be alone, in a hurry and in need, and do the feet wiping act to get into almost any home.

Whatever the story is, the homeowner buys the whole pretense and lets the stranger in. The criminal's buddies who were hiding in the bushes follow him in the door, and they immediately beat up and/or gag, blindfold and tie the homeowner and others up. Then the gang proceeds to burglarize the home. It is too easy.

In the days before cell phones, my aunt and uncle used to live in the Denver, Colorado area next to a busy street. People regularly rang their doorbell, hoping to gain entry on the pretense of their car being broken down and they needed to use their phone.

My aunt was instructed to not even open the door but to offer to call whatever phone number the person shouted to her through the door. Most of the strangers went away without having her dial a number, which means most of them were likely up to no good.

No verbal or physical power of suggestion was going to work on my aunt and uncle because they just flat out never opened their door to strangers!

They also had iron bars on their windows, which likely signaled there were things of value in the home (which there were). The bars were a fire hazard for a family with six children who wouldn't be able to escape through a window, but absolutely nobody entered that home who was not a known person.

Dating example - Body language psychology works in the dating scene too, but you need to be careful with it. If fact, it can either make or break the date. Here are some of the tricks people use to affect the opposite sex.

The power pose – Your posture will tell others how to perceive you, so a power pose is a move that some people use. Some people stick their chest out. Others do the seated CEO bit with their hands behind their head and their feet up on the desk. It needs to be natural, though. It boosts your confidence in yourself and tells that other person you are confident. If you are a man, it has been said that it even raises your testosterone level.

Lean in, and tilt head – To lean back tells the other person you are not interested, even if you are saying all of the right things. To slump your shoulders makes you look like you aren't paying attention. However, to lean in, tilt your head and gaze into the eyes of the person you are talking to shows that you are interested and are sensitive, which will positively affect the other person.

Eye contact – Good eye contact, if mutual, can show you like or love the person. If they don't return the gazing, either they don't feel the same for you or they are anxious, and you'll have to figure them out. They may just be shy and need more time. Staring at a person, however, can be intimidating or creepy.

Subtle movements – It is said that a woman rolling up her sleeves can be her way of attempting to be intimate. If she pulls a wine glass toward herself, she may be closing the gap that is between the two of you, which shows attraction. If she also plays with her necklace or hair, things are looking good!

A man who is flirting will do the triangle with his eyes, looking at both of the woman's eyes, then in her mouth, and then back up to the eyes. He may also put his shoulders back and breathe in.

Invading one's personal space – This move will either make you blow your first date with that special someone or else move it along into the direction you want it to go in. If they don't want you into their space, your being there will irritate them. If they do like you in their space, they'll interpret this move as liking, loving or stimulating them.

Err on the cautious side in a dating situation so as to not blow your chances with somebody you are interested in. Use body language to show your true feelings. It just needs to be respectful.

To know if they like you, you'll have to rely on the cues the other person gives you, such as a mutual leaning in, pointing their feet toward you, uncrossed legs, open arms, palms up, playing with their jewelry or hair, good eye contact, smiling or shyly looking down.

If your date puts space between you, leans away from you, points their feet away from you, crosses their legs and/or arms, closes their hands, rubs their eyes, scratches their nose, rubs the back of their neck, frowns, grimaces and/or looks to the side, there is a pretty good chance they are not keen on the idea of spending much more time with you.

As with reading people in other situations, you should look for clusters of behavior. See whether the person is doing several things in the positive list above or in the negative list above.

If they give you negative feedback, change your approach or else just wait. They either don't like what you are doing or what you are asking them. Being responsive to the situation will help you in the long run.

Chapter 6: The (Body) Language of Love

Once trained in reading body language, and specifically, where it relates to physical attraction, we can quickly know when somebody is physically attracted to us.

Knowing what that person is thinking will allow us to react quicker than other people do, either reciprocating the attraction or nipping it in the bud, as they say, without the other person embarrassing himself or herself too much.

A trained eye in the art of body language can also make fairly accurate assumptions about the love lives of couples and other people, which can be somewhat amusing.

Before we get into examples of men and women interacting, let's look at some of the better-known cues that men and women give to each other when they find themselves attracted to somebody.

The Body Language of Men

Leaning forward fully facing the woman – Attracted to the woman

Touching hair, but not twirling – Romantically interested in woman if also sending other signs of flirting

Hands lifted over their head, 90 degrees – Attracted to woman

The Body Language of Women

Raising eyebrows, lowering eyelids – Seducing the man

Gazing socially – Playing hard to get, looking between his two eyes and his mouth

Looking up, to the side – Telling the man, "Come hither."

Twirling hair – Interested romantically in the man if also sending other signs of flirting

Hair flicking – Interested romantically in the man if also sending other signs of flirting

Touching torso of own body – Attracted to the man

Touching on the man's body below the belt – Telling him not to forget her ... she will be back

The Body Language of an Unattached Man or a Woman

Blinking, lots of – Attracted to person (if not anxious or showing consternation, disagreement or consternation)

Eye contact across room with stranger - Attracted to person

Gazing regularly – Encouraging person to like the gazer

Gazing intimately – Showing they're having intimate thoughts, looking from eyes to mouth and the body

Gazing up and down – Attracted and appraising the sexuality of the other person

Glancing sideways – Flirting (if not uncertain or needing information)

Glancing sideways, raised brow – Flirting

Glancing for long periods, repeatedly – Sexual attraction, lustful if done from a distance

Looking away – Could be attracted to you (if not shy or curious about surroundings)

Pupils dilated – Aroused (if not just in low light or on substance)

Smiling too long – Attracted (if not just nervous, really happy or lying)

Smiling for no good reason while talking, sometimes suppressing it – Attracted to you

Smiles that take time to fade – Genuine attraction

Rubbing brows – This in general means that the person liked something. If this is always done in the presence of a particular person, the one making the gesture likes that person.

Hand palms up – Romantically interested

Feet are pointing toward the person ("orientation") – Attracted to the person that they face.

Foot or feet pointing toward the crowd or the door – Ready to leave the conversation.

Standing with weight on one leg and the other leg contently crossed – Content to stay for a while talking about that one.

Physical closeness – The one attracted to the other person gets into that other person's personal space, or at least closer than they do to other people.

Pointless chatter – The one who is attracted to another may ask questions he already knows the answer to, and the frequency of trivial requests to talk to you may increase.

Nice one day, cold the next – Strong sign of attraction. The person did not get the response they wanted and is pulling back from the person they are attracted to, covering their track.

Always where you are – Many coincidental meetings are not coincidental. The attracted person is either matching your schedule or is frequenting your same haunts just to run into you.

Befriending the friends of the love interest – The attracted person is getting into the other person's world and/or getting as close to the love interest as possible.

Cancellations – Making the love interest top priority.

Keeping an eye on love interest – The attracted person is making sure their target of amore is still there.

Couples Body Language

Physical touching and closeness – Showing affection

Physical touch avoidance – False statement; not feeling affectionate

Touching face when kissing – Slow seduction and genuine romantic interest

Social Setting

Let's say there is a group of single girls talking, and single men start to come into the room. There are certain "tells," to borrow a poker term that people give off that signal interest.

Ironically, it's the women that give off the first signal. Typically, it's hair flicking that girls will do first. It is a classic example of preening, which tells the guy to look at her hair and to look at her. Almost all of the girls in the group will do it one after the other because it is a contagious behavior that they actually mimic.

Then they may watch the incoming guy longer than what is normal, which the guy notices. Since courtship is almost always the female's choice, guys wait for the "approach tell." A long gaze and a smile will be interpreted as an approach tell.

If a strange guy approaches a group of girls that has not been given an approach tell, he'll stand there looking stupid and lost because the girls will pretend he is not there. Misinterpreting the approach tell or trying to fit in when a different guy had been given the approach tell can be embarrassing.

Girls may use their hair, mouth and their eyes to compete for or keep a man's attention. Another thing that women may do is to expose their neck, which is a flirtatious gesture that says they trust you not to harm them (because the neck is a vulnerable place).

A girl may even touch a guy high on his butt and on the side when she passes by to go somewhere. It is provocative and tells the guy not to forget her ... she'll be back. A guy will usually then watch for that girl to return.

In a standing position when all the weight is on one leg, and the other leg crosses it, this is not a negative sign but is a sign that the person is there for the long haul. They are interested in the conversation.

When they uncross their legs and one-foot points into the crowd or toward the door, the other person has lost them. Facial expressions are more controlled, and they may look away whenever they get the chance.

When a girl thinks she is losing a guy's attention, she'll preen herself again on the side away from wherever he is starting to put his attention. Then she may go for the "eye pop" where her eyes close and then pop open with a loving stare. She may tilt the head a little or give and exaggerated look of incredulity or a grimace.

A sideways hug reduces the intimacy of the hug and shows the others what she is doing. A pat on the back just before releasing seems friendly, but it is a release signal that says it's time to let go.

Girls who like a particular guy may stand next to him. If a different guy feels threatened, they may do the chin tuck, almost pouting. The girls may flirt with a guy they are not sexually interested in because girls view it as good manners, even if they don't mean it.

Guys notoriously misread the girls and stay confused. The girls say that it is the smiling they do that the guys always misinterpret as the "approach tell," when they could be looking around the room and smiling at what was being said rather than at a guy who is wishful thinking.

YouTube Examples

There are a couple of YouTube videos that show examples of celebrity men interacting with women. We'll pick on celebrities since they put themselves out there on camera for all to see.

One of them is not married but had a girlfriend at the time of this filming. He seemed to be trying to have a one-night stand with his interviewer. The next celebrity was (and remains) married, but there are many signs of some sort of marital problem.

David Cassidy

His career background - David Cassidy, who was the star of the 1970s sitcoms, "The Partridge

Family," was a huge heartthrob and teen idol to young girls all over the world. His first recording for the show came out before the show debuted. The song was "I Think I Love You," and it shot to number one on the American charts in just one week.

It also brought overnight fame to a guy who had just signed up for the show so that he could pay the rent. It wasn't long before David launched his own recording and concert career in his off hours. At one point, David was the highest paid entertainer on the planet, and his fan base was bigger than that of Elvis Presley, and the Beatles combined.

The romantic interest/mania of the girls - There is no question as to the romantic interests of his millions of fans. In fact, young girls did crazy things at David's concerts during the years of "Cassidymania," such as fainting, crying, and screaming his name out.

The mobs of girls pushed forward to be closer to David after he got onto the stage, trampling over the girls at the front who were between them and their idol. One girl in England had a heart attack and died in all the excitement at one of his concerts.

Sometimes David had to enter his concerts disguised as a paramedic or something else and leave hotels in laundry carts so as to not be noticed and mobbed. He hid in blankets until that no longer worked.

Limousines were turned over and destroyed when girls assumed he was in one of them, trying to force him to climb out so they could get close to him. Often, he was actually in the trunk of a Toyota and the limousines the girls destroyed were just decoys.

The mob situation at the better hotels caused David to be banned from staying in them, so he was often holed up in dumpy motels, unable even to go out to eat. David had to stay on a boat on the river in London because all of the city's hotels banned him there. Some entire countries banned him because of the teenage hysteria that followed him.

When successful at getting close to him in mob situations, girls scratched David or tore off pieces of his clothes, pulled out some of his hair, or snipped off some hair for souvenirs.

Whew, well there's no question of adoration on the part of millions of girls, although they were actually dangerous to him when they were in large numbers. If not for his thirty or so security people and the many creative military-style operations they invented so as to get him to and from concerts, he would have literally been "loved" to death!

There remains a remnant of David's fans to this day, which has made some commenters say that David's fans are just about the most devoted, die-hard group of rock star fans in history.

David's interest in women – During those Partridge Family years, David lived for women and rock and roll, but he also worked 18-hour days. It has been said that if there had been a child labor law in effect for 19-year-olds and 20-year-olds, they had violated it with David.

Still, there was no shortage of romantically interested girls and brief encounters in David's world, and this early experience taught David to expect all women to be "easy" to get into bed. Having a long-term relationship with a woman became a distant memory to him, and he stated many times on camera that it was actually "lonely at the top."

Girls were brought to his hotel rooms or his rented boat if in London. They came to his dressing room on the Partridge Family set, sometimes as welcomed guests and other times as small mobs who reached his dressing room.

The encounters often involved sex, and David tried to be sure that the girls were of legal age. He wasn't interested in young girls anyway. Most of his lovers were complete strangers to him, never to be seen again.

David quit the show and his touring while he was at the top of his fame because of exhaustion, the dangerous level of teenage hysteria that had formed, and because of the fact that he didn't have a life. He stated that by the time he quit the show and quit touring at about 25 years of age, he was emotionally still 19 years old, which was the age he was when he shot to fame and started to do nothing but work around the clock.

David, an interesting case study - One thing that makes David an interesting person for us to study is the fact that he was a modern-day Cassanova.

Over the years, his teenage fans grew into mature women who married and had kids. David was also married ... sometimes. He was not faithful to his wives, which caused many of his marital problems. Sometimes he even picked out love interests on camera while doing some sort of business (i.e. on a talk show, etc.), and other times he tried to hide his attempted trysts from the wives.

David's looks gradually changed and then faded in recent years. For various reasons, David's advances toward women have not always been accepted as they had usually been in his heyday.

Some of these rejections are on video and are now available on YouTube. As in the case study below, we can observe the body language of one uninterested recipient of his romantic advances.

Cassidy Case Study #1 (Type into YouTube: "Benezra 1")

The video footage – You will recall that in Chapter 2 we discussed the topic of perception and how one's background and culture play a part in the perceptions we have of situations. David didn't seem to always pay attention to what the cultural norms were in the various countries so as to alter his initial approach or his expectations of women. He just kept assuming that all women were interested in him sexually, as had been his early experience when he became famous.

The encounter in this footage was shot in Canada in 1990 when David Cassidy was 40 years old, still looking good, and his girlfriend and future wife, Sue Shifrin, was back at home, pregnant with their son, Beau.

A pretty French female interviewer had flown into the area of Canada where David was staying and promoting his new album, "Lying to Myself." The woman came to conduct an interview with David herself and also to film his radio interview. Of course, she had a cameraman traveling with her.

In the video, she was filmed greeting David Cassidy in his hotel room as he put his guitar down and greeted her. David light-heartedly asked why the cameraman was with her, and she gave a light-hearted answer.

Within just a short while, though, David appeared to be increasingly annoyed at continually being filmed talking to her in his hotel room. The footage was cut off and then was back on a couple of times. The woman finally ended the mild feud by just telling everyone it was time to leave the hotel.

The camera man filmed them getting into a limousine. Then he filmed them getting out of it at a radio station. David was the perfect gentleman where getting in and out of vehicles with a woman was concerned.

We next briefly see David talking on the radio about what he'd been doing for the 15 or so years that had passed since he walked away from the show and from touring. He also promoted the new album on the radio.

After his radio interview, filming continued inside the limousine for a brief time. Even though nobody was interviewing David there and he had a chance to ask the French woman about herself or to talk about subjects other than himself, David continued to talk about himself. He talked about becoming famous 20 years earlier with the release of his first hit song, "I Think I Love You." Not much footage was shot in the car.

Filming continued in a small public bar that was fairly empty. This was where they went to conduct their interview. There was no more footage of them in David's hotel room. If David thought to get this woman into bed back at the hotel, he was now going to have to get her interested in him during the interview in the bar!

They were both sitting on bar stools next to the bar. They were facing each other straight on and were leaning in toward each other slightly, though David kept one elbow on the bar. The woman actually leaned in more than David did at the very start of the interview.

They were sitting rather closely for an interview, according to normal American standards, but it was a normal proximity in French culture. Their faces were within two feet of each other. Both of them were comfortable with the close space.

Most of what went on from this point on from a body language perspective had to do with the interviewer resting her chin on her fist when David bored her and took her hand away when what David said interested her.

The French woman began her interview of David, asking just a few questions and letting David do most of the talking. She asked David what his dreams were for his life before he got involved with the Partridge Family.

Instead of answering her question directly and talking about his dreams, David talked about his bad behavior in his youth, saying he was a "pretty wild boy," who was kicked out of school three times, "undisciplined," and had "grown up with his mother." He said he had not been brought up by his famous stepmother, Shirley Jones, and his dad. Apparently, David thought the bad boy image would be a turn-on.

When the conversation went into that direction, the woman rested her chin on her fist and continued to listen. David then answered her question directly, mentioning his acting ambitions and his first professional job. When he did that, she dropped her hand from her chin and appeared to be more interested in what he was saying.

Then David talked of being on the Partridge Family and telling the teen magazines that he didn't want them to make him into a teen idol. The interviewer was impressed that at age 19 David could already see the direction things were going.

David said he knew girls were falling in love with the Keith Partridge character he portrayed on the show and that he was afraid of rejection if they ever got to know him personally because he was very different from the character he played.

The two seemed to connect during this part of the conversation, and David had no problems briefly placing a hand or two on her shoulders when he talked to her. He started to lean more toward her.

She, however, moved back and sat slightly more upright than she had been.

When David was presented with copies of some of the Partridge Family albums, all he had to say about them was how the records and the television show had created his identity crisis where people thought he was the show's character, Keith.

The interviewer again rested her chin on her fist and nodded her head while he talked about his identity crisis and complained about not being able to play and sing the kind of music he was interested in (while making nearly $8 million from singing them in concerts over those few years).

Naturally, the interviewer responded with a question about what kind of music that he preferred to record back then. He responded that he was into "much more serious rock-n-roll." Then the video cut to David's 1971 version of the song, "Cherish," which was soft music rather than hard rock and roll. Ironically, David recorded many more soft songs than hard ones over the years.

She asked him about whether women ever did get to know him ... basically asking him about his relationships after he was no longer cast as Keith Partridge and no longer worked long hours as he did in his heyday.

David shifted in his seat, obviously uncomfortable with the question. He responded with how he "was too busy to cultivate relationships."

With that response, the interviewer continued to rest her chin on her knuckles and nod. After all, she was talking to him at the age of 40, which was several years after his Partridge Family days and two failed marriages.

David adjusted his answer, explaining that he felt that his fame and success got in the way of women seeing him for himself. With that answer, she dropped her hand. He started leaning in toward her while continuing to tell her that people only saw his fame when they looked at him.

They were almost one foot apart from each other's face at that point in the conversation. David, for some reason, briefly put a hand on each of her shoulders and they both leaned in slightly toward each other.

She asked him about whether he "could end it" (the fame), to which he said he had ended it, retiring for a while after his 1975 world tour. Obviously, he was in the process of trying to revive his fame because he was in Canada to promote his new album. The interviewer put her fist back up under her chin and continued to nod while David talked about getting away from the madness.

David started to talk a lot about the huge numbers of people who were attending his concerts back in his heyday. He called his concerts "World War III," with young girls being laid out on stretchers and treated by paramedics and some going to the hospital. He said that his concerts had become "events," or "a thing," because of the young girls screaming while he was singing, getting hurt, destroying limousines, mobbing hotels to the point they banned him, etc.

His intention was for his concerts to be just a guy playing his guitar and singing and people enjoying his music. The interviewer dropped her fist again and was connecting with him throughout this part of the conversation.

She asked him about whether there was a specific date when he decided to retire, after which David briefly replied that he'd decided before the world tour that it would be the last time that he would tour for perhaps his whole life. He didn't have a direction, but he knew he needed to stop touring and to get a life.

Then the video abruptly ended. He may or may not have mentioned the death of the young teenager at Wembley Stadium while performing his farewell tour, but it is well-known that the death of that young concert attendee confirmed in David's mind that it was time to stop doing concerts. He felt guilt from it for years afterward.

The analysis – David knew there was going to be an interview, but he clearly did not expect the camera man to be with the interviewer and filming as early as their meeting in the hotel room.

David was dating Sue Shifrin back then. Sue was pregnant with David's son, Beau, and David likely did not want footage of him in a hotel room with a French woman to get back to her.

You hear the French woman ask David in his hotel if he was nervous about the interview and David replied that he was "over that" but that the cameraman was making him nervous (because he was filming in the hotel room).

David quite possibly had assumed that this French woman who had agreed to meet him at his hotel room was going to have sex with him. If David expected that, it does not seem that things with this French woman happened as David planned. In French culture, business meetings are kept formal and professional, especially in the beginning. Personal and private matters are kept separate from business.

In his interview with her, David was uncomfortable with the subject of deep, meaningful relationships, as was evident by his shifting in his seat when he was asked about whether or not women ever got to know him well.

Despite having had a few years since his heyday to form a meaningful relationship, he'd been married and divorced twice and had chronically cheated on his wives and girlfriends. Any signals he sent to this French woman were intended just for temporary pleasure.

David's constant use of the word, "I," and his non-stop talk about himself, whether or not he is in an interview, either means he is self-absorbed or depressed.

American men tend to lean in toward a woman and face them head on when they are attracted to them. David did this when they were conducting their interview in the bar, which was a dead give-away that he was indeed attracted to her and trying to connect with her. It could not be determined whether or not he used the triangle gaze on her.

The French woman mirrored David's behavior, facing him straight on. The physical closeness of these two was unusual by American standards, especially for an interview, but it was normal for the French, even in business meetings.

The interviewer likely wanted to appear congenial, so she mirrored his body language. It is possible that she was attracted to David, but she did not appear to want to be romantic with him.

David's touching both of her shoulders was unusual for an interview. He was likely wanting to see her reaction to his touching her (invading her space even more), but you'll notice that he never did it again during the interview.

The woman's body language (hand to chin, just nodding) throughout the interview showed that she was actually bored and faking interest in what David was saying for much of the interview. She exhibited this body language when David talked about being wild and undisciplined and whenever he complained endlessly about things that most other people would be envious of.

If you look into how the French think, you can understand why she became turned off during certain parts of the interview. American women often like "bad boys," but women in some other cultures do not. David's talk of being undisciplined, wild, etc., would not be impressive to a French woman because of the French value rational presentations, logical thought, integrity, and education.

This French woman's interest in what David had to say was piqued when he talked about his early career ambition to be an actor or his honest thoughts or his highly-attended concerts. This was evident by her hand being lowered from her face and her interjecting short comments or questions when he spoke of those kinds of things ... of excellence and honesty.

David seemed to be capable of reading her body language because he caught on whenever he was boring her, and he successfully adjusted his conversation to get her interested in the conversation again.

He may have misread her intentions when she agreed to meet him at his hotel, but I'm sure David has put into place once again after the interview if he pushed the issue!

Trump Case Study #1 (Type into YouTube: "Donald and Melania Trump's most awkward relationship moments")

There is just something weird about this married couple, at least to the American viewer. She very subtly thwarts all attempts on the president's part to display affection to Melania on camera. When he decides to be cool to her on camera, it is not subtle. He disrespects her in huge displays of disrespect.

Melania is from Slovakia, which is a country whose people are very formal. They follow protocols for every situation. To Slovakians, the family is everything. They are also private people who do not display affection publicly. Melania's background as a nude model seems to negate all of this, but as First Lady, Melania holds onto her upbringing of protocol and privacy.

President Trump is one of the leader types that we discussed in the first chapter. To a person with a leader personality, making money is the first priority and family comes second. The leader type typically enjoys showing off the things their wealth bought them, including their trophy wife.

President Trump has no problem displaying affection for his wife in public, which goes against her upbringing. As a showman, a playboy, a billionaire leader type with a trophy wife, and as an American, President Trump is just not prone to keep displays of affection for Melania private.

His only plausible excuse may be his phobia of descending stairs and wanting to get it over with quickly, but that excuse can't be used for much of what he does.

Let's take a deeper look at people who have the leadership personality. A person with the leader personality is in a hurry, so much so that they often interrupt people who make small talk so that they can get down to business. During the campaign months when the couple had interviews together, President Trump wouldn't let her speak. You'd see her start to talk and him taking over.

A leader may very well walk ahead of people, even his wife. The president recently also shoved aside a prime minister in a crowd and on camera so that he could stand in front of him.

Although leader personalities don't make family their first priority, Donald Trump always made his kids top priority when they were young and called him at work. No matter who Mr. Trump had in his office, he took the calls that came in from his kids.

Melania did not want her husband to become president, but he went ahead with that plan anyway. Now she is shoved further down his list of priorities.

Unlike first families before them, there is no public display of affection for each other going on, even just for the cameras. The president wants to show off his "trophy wife" and hold her hand, but she won't hold his hand in public.

According to one former secret service agent, the Clintons used to fight like crazy on an elevator and then walk off of the elevator looking like a loving couple for the cameras. Hillary even threw things at Bill and hit him on occasion behind the scenes. There was one time when he had a black eye. When she lost the election for president for the second time, Bill was missing in action!

We know the Obamas also had marital problems, but they always put on a good public display of mutual affection.

Not so with the Trumps. We appear to be witnessing their true relationship on the various videos, which makes them good case study material. This first video contains nine short clips of some of the Trumps' most awkward moments that were caught on camera. We'll talk about just seven of the clips here, starting with the third clip in the video.

Clip #3 – When the Trumps met the Obamas at the White House on President Trump's inauguration day, President Trump walked up the steps and greeted the Obamas before Melania had even made it out of the vehicle and around the back of it.

In contrast to President Trump, Mr. Obama looked for Melania after he greeted the president, helped Melania up the steps that she was trying to maneuver in high heels (and while holding a present she brought for Michelle), and he kissed her once on each cheek, as was the custom in Slovakia.

This video doesn't show it, but just after that fiasco, President Trump also walked into the White House in front of Melania and everyone else, still acting as if Melania wasn't with him or didn't matter. Mr. Obama, however, let both Melania and his wife walk ahead of him.

Analysis – There really are no words to defend the president's actions toward Melania on this day and especially in this clip. He and Melania appear to be in some sort of power struggle wherein he punishes her independence and refusal of public affection by showing independence of her and lack of affection in exaggerated ways.

The president may have been in a hurry and/or a little nervous, but he needed to stop himself and do the gentlemanly things for the cameras on a day when the entire world was watching!

Clip #4 – Melania and her son put a hand on their heart when the national anthem was being played at the White House Easter Egg Roll Day, but Melania had to nudge President Trump to put his hand up to his heart.

He knew what the nudge was for and immediately put his hand on his heart. He even patted his heart as if to assure the people that he really loves his country.

Analysis – The president's son had obviously been coached by Melania and was therefore prepared to put his hand on his heart.

President Trump did not react badly to Melania nudging his hand to remind him to put his hand on his heart. He almost looked like he did it on purpose and enjoyed annoying her, knowing it would bother her sense of protocol and that she would catch him.

This interaction between them shows a comfort level between Donald and Melania, as well as showing how closely Melania watches the behavior and protocol of her family.

Clip #5 – On inauguration day, President Trump turned around and faced his family while Rev. Billy Graham's son spoke.

Melania thought her husband was sharing his inauguration moment with her, and she smiled at him. But he looked past her and said something to his daughter, Ivanka, who was standing behind and to the side of Melania. Melania's smile dropped and turned into a hurt expression.

Analysis - This clip went viral on social media because, with one sentence, President Trump turned his wife's smile into a huge frown. After a few weeks, people realized he wasn't speaking to Melania, but to Ivanka, who could be seen reacting favorably to her dad talking to her.

President Trump was sharing the moment with Ivanka and leaving Melania out of his special moment. President Trump has always put the kids he had with Ivana before any wife. Melania was clearly hurt by being ignored and passed over in favor of speaking to his daughter on his special day.

Clip #6 – In another clip of the Trumps at the top of stairs and coming down from an airplane, Melania came out of the plane first and then politely waited for President Trump to come out. She turned to face the steps when he came out, and he took the opportunity to grab her hand when she wasn't looking. Melania very quickly and almost unnoticeably flicked her wrist to get her hand out of his. They stood and waved at everyone and then descended the stairs.

Analysis – This is yet another time when Melania wouldn't Americanize and hold her husband's hand in public.

Clip #7 – They "air kissed" on what appears to be inauguration day. The casual viewer may not notice that their lips did not touch any part of the face of the other person, but the slow-motion recap in this clip reveals they didn't actually kiss.

Analysis – It seems odd that a woman who won't hold hands has any problem kissing in public, however, a brief look at Slovakian culture reveals that friends and relatives greet each other with a kiss on both cheeks.

Melania looked both surprised and amused at the missed kiss, so maybe Mr. Trump stopped short of actually kissing her. This may be part of the power struggle they appear to be having regarding her independence and refusal to display affection for him publicly.

It is quite possible, however, that this was genuinely a missed kiss where each of them thought the other one would do the actual kiss on a cheek while they held their mouth in a kiss pose.

Clip #8 – At the inauguration dance, the president said something in Melania's ear that surprised her and made her head go back a little to look at him. He mirrored her head movement and smiled.

Analysis – It clearly amused the president to say something shocking to her.

Clip #9 – In this clip of the inauguration, Melania was escorted to where President Trump was standing. He noticed her, but they didn't hold hands. Immediately after that, Michelle joined Barack who was already smiling when she arrived.

Barack animatedly grabbed Michelle's hand and kissed it while Michelle remained looking at her escort, unaffected by Barack's kiss. Melania saw the kiss of Michelle's hand. President Trump looked over again at them just after the kiss.

Analysis President Trump didn't bother to try to hold Melania's hand this time, which was unusual for him. Mr. Obama likely knew they are all on camera, and he always shows affection for Michelle on camera.

Watching the scene closely, one notices that Barack was smiling for no apparent reason just before Michelle was escorted to him. The lifting of Michelle's hand to kiss it was overly animated so as to be noticed. Michelle appeared indifferent to his kissing her hand as if it happened all the time. It appeared to be done to show the contrast between the couples.

Trump Case Study #2 (Type into YouTube: "Melania Trump Not Allowed in Donald's Side of The Car - Sad!")

In this video, the commentator ignored the president's social blunder on the tape that her station was rolling while she spoke of the president's visit to West Palm Beach, Florida.

In the footage, the president bounded down the steps from the airplane. Acting like a young boy, he was about three or four steps ahead of Melania and then hurried into an SUV that was parked at the bottom of the stairs. He got in on the side of the vehicle that was not visible to the camera.

We can't see what exactly happens when Melania tried to get into the vehicle, but it is obvious that she had expected to get in it after the president did because both of them disappeared while they were close to the vehicle.

A man is seen briefly hurrying down the steps at the time Melania was trying to get into the vehicle. Then he stopped hurrying as she came back into view.

Melania walked around the back of the vehicle by herself to get into the SUV on the side that faces the camera. Whether or not she opened the door for herself was not shown.

Analysis – This was deliberate disrespect for the First Lady. Melania, by all reports, is an independent soul, so it may be that she takes her independence too far for President Trump and he finds ways to make fun of her independence publicly.

There really is no excuse for any husband to act like this, though, and for an American president, this kind of behavior is unheard of.

Chapter 7: Rewards of Successful Analysis

The rewards of knowing how to read body language are significant because it is an effective extension of communication. Words are just not enough.

The following are five specific benefits to learning this skill:

1. *Connect better with people* – Between 60 and 93% of in-person communication is done through the non-verbal cues ... body language, yet we concentrate on the words that we say and not on what our body says.

   Even if you mirror a tiny gesture the other person makes, that person will connect better with you. If you don't tower over a small person when you deliver harsh news, your message will be better received. There are many examples of things you can do to get your message across in a better manner than words alone can do.

2. *Improve your business* – If you are making sales of any kind in person, you will do well to read the other person's body language to see how your message is being received.

If the person you are talking to is folding their arms, crossing their ankles, turning away from you, etc., you know they are closed down, and your spoken message is not affecting them in the way you want it to.

If you know from their body language that your message is not being received well, you can find out what the objections are and try to overcome them. Make them see. Solve all of their problems. This open dialogue paves the way for better sales for you and customer satisfaction for the customers.

3. *Prevents conflict* – People make statements with their body language when they are mad, even before they speak about what they are thinking. If you read those messages and adjust what you say, you can prevent arguments in many cases.

4. *Improve your presence* – Once you become knowledgeable about body language, you will start to notice your own body language and begin to make changes to it. When you make changes, you send out a different message.

   For example, you may notice yourself slouching and begin to improve your posture. Others will think you to be confident.

   Not only do you affect others when you change how you hold yourself, but you change yourself. Consciously make a few changes to your body language, and you will start to make yourself feel that way.

It is interesting to note that ballroom dance students subconsciously start to improve their posture when they are not on the dance floor and start to give off an impression of confidence in general. That is because part of what is taught in ballroom dancing is posture and they are thinking about it and practicing it a lot. Learning any physical skill like dance moves or karate gives a person extra confidence.

5. *Open up your world* – Once you know body language, you will suddenly be able to see it everywhere you go.

You will be able to observe a social gathering of people and see all sorts of nonverbal messages that people send with their bodies. You can see who is making whom nervous, who is attracted to whom, who is enjoying their conversation and who wants to leave the event at the first chance.

Chapter 8: The Art of Reading Body Language

Once you have the personality type of a person you are reading figured out, certain personality traits can be expected. Sometimes there is a secondary personality type that you will notice.

While you can figure out a lot about a person from their personality type and background information that you can gather, there is always that odd fellow who just breaks the mold.

President Trump should be used to foreign wives by now, but Slovakian wife Melania Trump appears to be too independent for his taste, and he appears to publicly punish her for doing things her own way, even to the point of making himself look bad with his antics.

A foreign person's cultural, social norms could be far different from American social norms, which could cause misunderstandings or even exasperation with a situation. Therefore, some body language means something different than what Americans think it does. Other body language elements are universal.

As we saw in the David Cassidy interview, the French will cozy up with Americans for an interview and even meet you in your hotel room. But, you won't be conducting any monkey business with a French person who is on assignment doing legitimate business, even if you are David Cassidy and just wanting a one-night stand!

Most of us have ancestry from various countries, which says that our ancestors managed to figure out the (body) language of love, possibly even before they could speak the same language!

It is good to study the various gestures, gazes, etc., so as to read people in general and also to read a love interest. Once you have that mastered, you can quickly adjust your message, just as if they had spoken what their body said.

Remember that people often speak one thing, and their body language says something else. Believe the body language in those cases.

In addition to reading people, you can apply some of these body language poses, mirroring and other gestures, the power of suggestion movements, etc., to convey your message more effectively. Knowing what to do with your body when you speak will help you get your messages across and get people to connect with you and do what you want them to do more often.

Additional Books by Author

For the next book in the series go to
http://bit.ly/asmith-books